CONTENTS

PART I   REGISTRATION

PART II   LIBRARIES

PART III   ARCHIVES

INTRODUCTION

This book is intended for those of us researching our roots in the north east of Scotland. In the last thirty years there has been a tremendous growth of interest in family history research. This led, in January 1987, to the opening of the Family History Society's premises in King Street. There you can search your north east roots and your roots in other parts of the world. This publication is a guide to the sources available to the researcher in the north east of Scotland. Anyone researching their family history in Aberdeen now has access to a tremendous amount of information and hardly needs to leave the city to discover most of the information necessary to their search.

Given the nature of this guide it will go out of date very quickly with office moves, increasing costs etc, hopefully these will be minor irritations. Every effort has been made to check information, and details are as accurate as they currently can be in February 2008. All opinions in this booklet are those of the author and not of the Family History Society.

My thanks must go to everyone who is involved with these libraries and archives who gave up their time to help with this book. Without them there would be no book and no ease of research for us all. My special thanks to the late Mrs Sheila Beverly who not only drew all the maps but gave many helpful suggestions on earlier editions, to Mrs Jean Shirer for pushing, prodding and helping me to put together this fifth edition, to Stuart West, Margaret Ewing and Bill Diack for providing the photos. Lastly but not least to my family, husband Bill and children Fiona, Shonagh, Andrew and Calum for putting up with me, my foibles and my passion for family history and for growing up with north east roots!!

LESLEY DIACK
February 2008

SOME ABBREVIATIONS USED

ANESFHS	-	Aberdeen & North East Scotland Family History Society
c.	-	circa
IGI	-	International Genealogical Index
IRCs	-	International reply paid coupons
LDS	-	(Church of Jesus Christ of) Latter Day Saints
MIs	-	Monumental Inscriptions
ms	-	Manuscript
OPRs	-	Old Parochial Registers
P	-	Parking
PC	-	Personal computer
SAE	-	Stamped Addressed Envelope

THE REGISTRATION SYSTEM

In Scotland there is a copy of all the Registers of Births, Deaths and Marriages from 1855 (the start of Civil Registration) to date in New Register House in Edinburgh. However, sets are also held in area repositories but these are not usually complete to the present day. There are 2 larger area repositories in the north east - Aberdeen and Elgin. In the following pages there are maps and details on each of the repositories. After that, there is a list of the smaller, often part-time. registrars who hold the more modern records. Those registrars without addresses are usually part-time and often work from home.

Other than the physical amount of information held, the main differences between Edinburgh and an area repository is in the index. In Edinburgh there is a computerised cumulative whole of Scotland index split by year and sex. In the area repository it is split by parish and year and is not cumulative even for the parish, although in some repositories, for a small charge, access is available to the computer system in Edinburgh. If this is not available you will therefore need to be fairly sure of a parish or you could have a lot of searching, but sometimes that is part of the fun. Information held on Scottish certificates is as follows:-

BIRTH Name, when and where born, sex, name and occupation of father, name and maiden name of mother, date of their marriage (except 1856-60), name, relationship and address of informant, when and where registered. Other children of parents and parents' age and place of birth (1855 only).

MARRIAGE When and where married, how married, name and occupation of bride and groom, marital status and relationship (if any), ages of bride and groom (1855 only; birthplace, where/when registered), usual residence, names and occupation of both sets of parents and whether alive or dead, names of minister, registrar and witnesses, when and where registered, number of children by any other marriages (1855 only).

DEATH Name and occupation of the deceased and marital status, when/ where died, age, names and occupations of parents and whether alive or dead, cause of death and name of doctor who certified death; name residence and relationship of informant (name only in 1855), when and where registered and signature of registrar, place of birth and length of time in district (1855 only), spouse's name if married (omitted 1856-60), issue in order of birth, names and ages (1855 only), burial place and name of undertaker (1855-

REGISTRAR OF BIRTHS, DEATHS & MARRIAGES
ABERDEEN

The Registrar in Aberdeen has paper copies of the birth certificates to 1899 and marriage and death certificates to 1939 for Aberdeen city, Aberdeen county and Kincardine county. They also have on microfiche the certificates for birth, marriage and death to 1967 for the same areas and access to the computerised, whole of Scotland index and digital images.

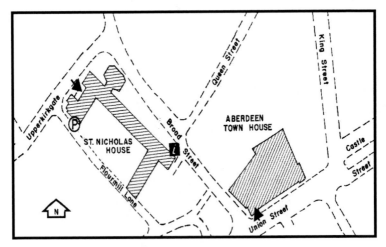

REGISTRAR OF BIRTHS, DEATHS & MARRIAGES
ST NICHOLAS HOUSE
UPPERKIRKGATE
ABERDEEN   AB10 1BA
Tel: (01224) 523340 (ask for search supervisor)

UPPERKIRKGATE ENTRANCE

OPENING TIMES

MONDAY - THURSDAY   9.15am-4.45pm
FRIDAY   9.15am-4.30pm

NB   Closes at lunchtime for 1 hour (12.30pm-1.30pm). A search supervisor is there to handle the material, help researchers, and take bookings.

MUST BOOK IN ADVANCE with search supervisor.

COST: £10 for one hour's search. £13.50 per certificate (during day's search this is reduced to £8.50). An abbreviated birth certificate costs the same as a full one. The cost is £15 per hour for a computer search of Scottish indexes and digital images.

FACILITIES FOR DISABLED: Enter by podium on corner of Broad Street (Rent Office entrance). Please notify office in advance.

WRITTEN ENQUIRIES ARE ACCEPTED

REGISTRAR OF BIRTHS, DEATHS & MARRIAGES
ELGIN

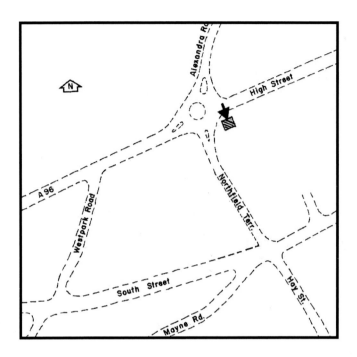

ELGIN REGISTRAR
240 HIGH STREET
ELGIN
IV30 1BA
Tel: (01343) 554600
Fax: (01343) 554644
Email: heather.greig@moray.gov.uk

OPENING TIMES

MONDAY - FRIDAY   9.00am - 4.00pm

Appointment system in operation.

COST: £5 for fifteen minutes. £13.50 per certificate (during day's search this is reduced to £8.50). An abbreviated birth certificate costs the same as a full one. Access to DIGROS – Digital Imaging of the Genealogical Records of Scotland's People.

FACILITIES FOR DISABLED - on ground level.
WRITTEN ENQUIRIES DEALT WITH - PLEASE ENCLOSE S.A.E

REGISTRATION IN THE NORTH EAST

ABOYNE District Council Office Bellwood Road Aboyne AB34 5HQ Tel 01339 886109 aboyne.registrar@aberdeenshire.gov.uk Registration opening hours: Mon-Fri 8.45 to 1.00 & 2.00 to 4.30	**ALFORD** Council Office School Road Alford AB33 8PY Tel 01975 562421 alford.registrar@aberdeenshire.gov.uk Registration opening hour Mon-Fri 8.45 to 12.30 & 1.30 to 4.30
BALLATER Mrs Mary Croll An Creagan 5 Queens Road Ballater AB35 5NJ Tel 01339 755535 Registration by appointment only	**BANCHORY** The Square High Street Banchory AB31 5RW Tel 01330 822878 banchory.registrar@aberdeenshire.gov.uk Registration opening hours Mon-Fri 9.00 to 12 noon & 2.00 to 4.30
BANFF Seafield House 37 Castle Street Banff AB45 1FQ Tel 01261 813439 banff.registrar@aberdeenshire.gov.uk Registration opening hour Mon-Fri 9.00 to 12.30 & 1.30 to 4.30	**BRAEMAR** Mrs Alice Cumming Braemar Royal Highland Society Hall Hillside Road Braemar AB35 5YU Tel 013397 41349 Mob 07990 657638 Registration by appointment only
ELLON Area Office 29 Bridge Street Ellon AB41 9AA Tel 01358 726401 ellon.registrar@aberdeenshire.gov.uk Registration opening hours Mon-Fri 9.00 to 12 noon & 2.00 to 4.30	**FRASERBURGH** 14 Saltoun Square Fraserburgh AB43 9DA Tel 01346 513281 fraserburgh.registrar@aberdeenshire.gov.uk Registration opening hours Mon-Fri 8.45 to 12.30 & 1.30 to 5.00
HUNTLY 25 Gordon Street Huntly AB54 8AN Tel 01466 794488 huntly.registrar@aberdeenshire.gov.uk Registration opening hours Mon-Fri 8.45 to 12.30 & 1.30 to 4.30	**INSCH** Mrs Frances Mitchell Marbert George Street Insch AB52 6JL Tel 01464 820964 Registration by appointment only

INVERURIE Gordon House Blackhall Road Inverurie AB51 3WA Tel 01467 628011 inverurie.registrar@aberdeenshire.gov.uk Registration opening hours Mon-Fri 8.45 to 12.30 & 1.30 to 4.45	MAUD Council Offices Nethermuir Road Maud AB42 4ND Tel 01771 613667 maud.registrar@aberdeenshire.gov.uk Registration opening hours Mon-Th 8.45 to 12.30 & 1.30 to 5.00 Fri 8.45 to 12.30 & 1.30 to 4.00
*PETERHEAD Arbuthnot House Broad Street Peterhead AB42 1DA Tel 01779 493244 peterhead.registrar@aberdeenshire.gov.uk Registration opening hours Mon-Fri 9.00 to 12.30 & 2.00 to 4.30	STONEHAVEN & EAST KINCARDINE Viewmount Arduthie Road Stonehaven AB39 2DQ Tel 01569 768360 stonehaven.registrar@aberdeenshire.gov.uk Registration opening hours Mon-Fri 9.00 to 12.30 & 2.00 to 4.30
TURRIFF Towie House Manse Road Turriff AB53 4AY Tel 01888 562427 turriff.registrar@aberdeenshire.gov.uk Registration opening hours Mon-Fri 9.00 to 12.30 & 1.30 to 4.30	

Entries marked with * also hold Graveyard Information.

NB   These offices hold births from c.1900 and deaths and marriages from
c.1940 for their areas.

*ABERCHIRDER	(01466)780735
BUCKIE	(01542) 832691
BUCKSBURN, 23 Inverurie Road	(01224) 712866
FORRES, Auchernack, 153 High St	(01309) 694070
GRANTOWN-ON-SPEY	(01479) 872539
INVERBERVIE, Church Street	(01561) 361255
KEITH	(01542) 885525/6
LAURENCEKIRK, Royal Bank Buildings	(01561) 377245
OLDMELDRUM, Gordon Cott., Urquhart Cott.	(01651) 873028
PETERCULTER, North Deeside Road	(01224) 732648
*PORTSOY, 2 Main Street	(01261) 843843/842510
ROSEHEARTY	(01346) 513281
SAUCHEN	(01330) 833254
SKENE AND ECHT	(01224) 743371
STRATHDON, Old Engine House, Candacrale	(019756) 51226
TARVES	(01651) 842253
TORPHINS, Willowbank, Kincardine o'Neil	(013398) 84308

ABERDEEN CITY LIBRARIES

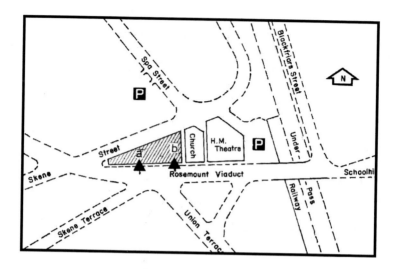

ABERDEEN CITY LIBRARIES
CENTRAL LIBRARY
ROSEMOUNT VIADUCT
ABERDEEN   AB25 1GW

Tel: (01224) 652500 (Switchboard)
Tel: (01224) 652512 (Local Studies)
Fax: (01224) 641985
Email: LocalStudiesLibrary@aberdeencity.gov.uk
Website: www.aberdeencity.gov.uk/libraries
(contact details for branch libraries and the library catalogue)

OPENING TIMES
Information Centre/Local Studies
MONDAY - THURSDAY: 9am - 8pm
FRIDAY & SATURDAY: 9am - 5pm

Lending and Children's Department, Media Centre
MONDAY - THURSDAY: 9am - 7pm
FRIDAY & SATURDAY: 9am - 5pm

Photocopying - 10p per A4 sheet : 20p per A3 sheet
Microfilm/fiche printouts - 10p each per A4 sheet: 20p per A3 sheet
Printing from PC – 20p per A4 sheet

There is no need to book, but it is advisable to contact the library in advance of any visit to ensure that material will be readily available for you. Some material is kept off site.

FACILITIES FOR DISABLED - contact staff (ramped Access and Lifts)

Written enquiries can be dealt with - please enclose an S.A.E or 2 x IRCs (Only a limited amount of research can be undertaken)

COMPUTER ACCESS: This is free but certain PCs in the Information centre are mainly for local and family history research. The PCs also give access to a range of online databases including The Times Digital Archive, The Oxford Dictionary of National Biography, NewsUK and SCRAN. Free access to the Ancestry website is also available on the PCs in the Information Centre and Media Centre. Access to Scotland's People website will also become available soon through a voucher scheme.

BUSINESS/TECHNICAL DEPARTMENT: Do not enter by the main entrance but by the door farthest from the theatre (entrance 'a' on map). Here you will find their collection of telephone directories which covers not only Scotland but Britain and America, Canada, Denmark, etc i.e. many of the places our ancestors came from and went to. Many an enjoyable day can be spent tracing "relatives" worldwide.

LENDING DEPARTMENT: This is on the ground floor at the main entrance (entrance 'b' on map). Library members are allowed to borrow 10 books for four weeks at a time. Membership is restricted to those who live in Aberdeen City. There is a small genealogical lending section under 929 (Dewey Classification). They also hold books on clans, surnames and placenames, Scottish and Local History, social life and conditions.

INFORMATION CENTRE: This is on the second floor. There is a large reference section on genealogy with both "How To" books and books on specific families. Black's *Surnames of Scotland* is also kept. The Dewey Classification here is 929 also. Other books of use are the *Fasti Ecclesiae Scoticanae* - records of Church of Scotland ministers - and the year books of the other churches in Scotland. There are also reference books on many related topics e.g. army records, navy records, gravestone inscriptions (rest of Scotland) etc. They have a great deal of material held in a store that can be fetched on request.

LOCAL STUDIES DEPARTMENT: This is also on the second floor part of the Information Centre. Here they have several 'fiche' and 'film readers which can be used to access the OPRs and Census 1841 - 1891 for Aberdeen City and Shire as well as Banffshire and Kincardineshire. They also have the OPR Index for Aberdeenshire, Banffshire and Kincardineshire. They are the only library in the area to hold the 'Given Name' Index as well as the OPR surname index. Sometimes if your ancestor is called SMITH it might be easier to check under his given name of say, Zebediah to find him rather than his surname. They also have the city newspapers on microfilm. The Library's main newspaper collection is held at Woodside. However there is no reader access. Any requests for material from the newspapers must be made to Local Studies.

The Local Studies section is full of material relating to Aberdeen City and Shire. There are directories, local histories, indexes, published records, gravestone inscriptions, 'In Memoriam' books, etc. They also have a large card index which can be checked for references to articles in journals and pamphlets. Much of their stock, for space reasons, is kept downstairs and often if you do not see what you want, just ask and it can be brought up for you. They also have an incomplete set of Valuation Rolls and Voters Rolls. There are many useful maps from the 19th century and earlier. None of this material may be borrowed.

There is also a collection of about 15,000 photographs ranging from 19th century prints to modern aerial views of the city.

The library also maintains a newspaper cuttings section where they collect relevant information on a variety of topics. If you are interested in a local business, shop or person they will have a copy of newspaper cuttings in one file. This can be very useful not just for family history but also for local history.

They do have some archival sources as well. For example the Aberdeen Footdee Society Minute Book exists for the late eighteenth and early nineteenth century. Here are listed the names of those who paid into the local Friendly Society and those who also received money from the fund. A very useful source if you have ancestors in Footdee.

The Public Library is a super place to do research. There is a wealth of local sources and some national, but they can be very busy especially during the summer. There is no need to book, but time limits operate when there are others waiting. On a Saturday it can often be difficult to get a seat or to photocopy.

There are seventeen branch libraries in the City, details of these can be found online. They are very much satellite departments of the main library and are unlikely to hold anything too different, but this can be checked using the online catalogue.

MORMON GENEALOGICAL LIBRARY

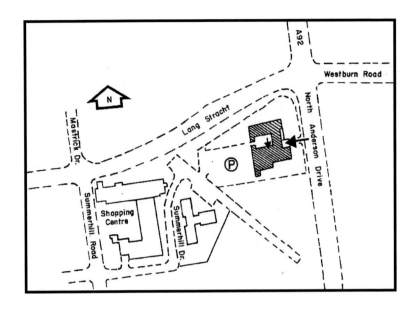

FAMILY HISTORY CENTRE
CHURCH OF JESUS CHRIST OF THE LATTER DAY SAINTS
NORTH ANDERSON DRIVE
ABERDEEN   AB15 6DD

Tel: (01224) 692206 (only phone during opening times)

OPENING TIMES

TUESDAY, WEDNESDAY AND THURSDAY	10.30am - 3.30pm
	7.00pm - 9.00pm
SATURDAY	10.30am - 12.30pm

Better to book in advance to reserve 'fiche/film reader or computer. No charge
unless film needs to be ordered, then from about £2.70 per film administration
charge, for a loan of one month. Donations gratefully received and these are put
towards expanding their library.

Printout and downloading facilities available (Disks available from the Centre).

COSTS: Computer Printouts - 10p : Reader Printouts - 30p : Disks – 40p
Manned by volunteer staff
PENCILS ONLY TO BE USED   :   FACILITIES FOR DISABLED
WRITTEN ENQUIRIES DEALT WITH - PLEASE ENCLOSE S.A.E. or 2x IRCs

The library is in the heart of the Mormon Church. There is a large car park at the back. you walk into the courtyard and enter by a door on your right hand side. On the first visit it is a bit difficult to find as it is a short distance from the back entrance and not well signposted. You can also enter by the main door at the front of the church. Usually there are people around to ask directions. It is a small room packed with PCs, microfilm and fiche readers. They can cope with 5 or 6 people maximum.

They have several indexes - the most recent IGI for the UK, the Family Registry Index (a sort of gigantic Directory of Interests), Parish and Vital Listings Index and their Locality Listings. The last two indexes are of little use to the amateur genealogist and can be a little confusing. They also hold a small stock of microfilm for the area by way of OPR and Census films. However, this is the place to do research outwith the area by using their ordering system to get films from all over Britain and the World. For about £2.70 per film they can get on loan for you an OPR for Perthshire, Census for London, Merchant Seaman's records, Civil Registration certificates, the list is endless. The problem is - how long to wait? It can be as short as 2-3 weeks or as long as 3 months or more. This depends on what is in stock in the Mormon British Headquarters in Birmingham. The other type of film that can be of use is the Nonconformist records. Not everyone had Church of Scotland ancestors and the Library can access on film such incongruous items as Portsoy Episcopal Records, Original Secession Records of Auchinleck, Ayrshire, Charlotte Street United Presbyterian in Aberdeen, etc.

I was disappointed by the lack of information there as they cannot hope to compete with the public library, ALIS, or The Family History Shop for coverage of the area with OPRs and Census but they can outshine them all by concentrating on the other sources of introduction such as Civil Registration, Non Conformists and other areas of Britain.

Once you have used their indexes to decide where your ancestors came from then it is best to order the relevant Census or OPR film. You have to fill out a slip with your name, address etc., the film you want, its unique number (available from the locality listing) e.g. Trinity Gask, Perthshire OPRs = 1040141, and hand it to one of the volunteers. Then it's just a matter of waiting and hoping.

They also have a very small published book library but this is mainly Family History Society publications with a few other minor sources.

A major development for the Library and for Aberdeen is the arrival of the CD Rom for the IGI. This is slightly more up to date than the 'fiche and information can be downloaded on to disk and then the researcher can play around with it to his or her heart's content.

ABERDEEN UNIVERSITY LIBRARY

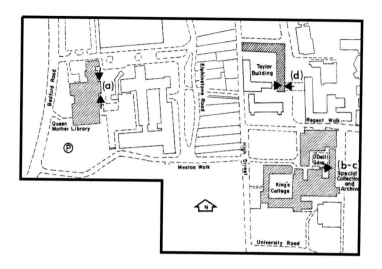

ABERDEEN UNIVERSITY LIBRARY

(a) **QUEEN MOTHER LIBRARY (QML)**
Meston Walk
ABERDEEN   AB24 3UE

Tel: (01224) 273600
Fax: (01224) 273956
Email: library@abdn.ac.uk
Website: www.abdn.ac.uk/library/

OPENING TIMES   Term Time
MONDAY - THURSDAY   9.00am - 10.00pm
FRIDAY   9.00am - 8.00pm
SATURDAY   9.00am - 10.00pm
SUNDAY   11.00am - 10.00pm
For vacation opening times please check www.abdn.ac.uk/library/hours.shtml

Photocopying, self-service by copycard at £2, £5 etc on sale in Library.
Online access to library catalogue - www.abdn.ac.uk/library/catalogue.shtml

Any member of the public can use the facilities of the Library. You must provide
proof of identity including your address before an access pass can be issued.
External users of the library can borrow material by paying the relevant fees.

FACILITIES FOR THE DISABLED.

b) SPECIAL LIBRARIES AND ARCHIVES

The Reading Room
O'Dell Garden
King's College
ABERDEEN   AB24 3SW

Tel: (01224) 272598
Fax: (01224) 273891
Email: speclib@abdn.ac.uk

OPENING TIMES
MONDAY - FRIDAY   9.30am - 4.30pm

No need to book, but advisable to make contact in advance.
Security procedure: signing in register, bags are deposited in the Reading Room
Office. Only pencil is used in the Reading Room.
Photocopying service at the discretion of the staff:
Flat bed photocopying - 12p per A4/24p per A3 for members/ 20p/40p for others
Scanned copies   - 30p per A4 sheet for members /60p for external readers
                              - 60p per A3sheet for members/£1 for external readers

QUEEN MOTHER LIBRARY

The key to the library is in its catalogue, which is online. It contains material held
in all sections of the library, including outlying branches, such as the Medical
Library, Law Library and Special Libraries and Archives. There are terminals
throughout the library. You can look for an item by author, or other name, by
title, or by keyword in a title. The computer terminals are also gateways to the
catalogues of many other university libraries.

BASEMENT

The basement is where all pre-1960 periodicals are housed, for example *Lloyds
Register of Shipping* (PER 380 LLO - lists of ships 1741-1826, who owned them,
captained them and where they went in particular years) or the Scottish Record
Society's Publications - PER 920 SCO. There are over 100 publications by this
Society covering subjects such as Edinburgh marriages, Aberdeen Testaments,
Caithness OPRs. A wealth of information usually all indexed and little used by
family historians.
There are *The List and Index Society* publications giving sources in England as
well. Also the Register of the Privy Council and the Spalding Club publications
and .... - the list just could go on and on! In short, all the Scottish Historical
Clubs and their publications are to be found here. But if your interests venture
south of the border there are English Historical Clubs with their records e.g.
Lancashire Quarter Sessions Records or London parish registers.

Down in the basement are also to be found the Indexes to the Sasines and Deeds
completed by the Scottish Record Office. For early family history there are also
the Privy Council records, the Records of Charters, the Records of the Privy Seal
and the Royal Treasurer. All of these are indexed and are a good starting point for
trying to trace people in the 15th and 16th centuries especially if you are tracing
a name rather than individuals.

FIRST FLOOR

This is where you find the general history books and valuable source books such
as the Statistical Accounts. Up here too among the Social Sciences there are
many books on the Army (with individual regimental histories), on the sea and
seafarers, on railways and railway companies etc. There is also a genealogy

section, which is small but houses family histories, 'how to' books, monumental inscriptions etc. There are also guides to genealogy world wide, not just in Scotland. Another useful source is The National Inventory of Documentary Sources on microfiche. This reproduces the descriptive lists of manuscript holdings of many repositories throughout the country, indexed. It is incomplete, but still very useful.

SPECIAL LIBRARIES AND ARCHIVES

Aberdeen University Library has its origins in the foundation of King's College in 1495 and Marischal College in 1593. This Department is responsible for all the pre-1841 publications and other special printed material held by the Library, as well as for the University Archives, plus many collections of estate, family and personal papers, and archives of organisations. The Local Collection contains printed material of all periods on all subjects relating to north east Scotland arranged first geographically, then by subject. A particular strength of the Local Collection is, of course, material relating to the University, e.g. books listing graduates.

One of the main primary sources for the family historian is an index to the *Aberdeen Journal* from its start in 1747 till 1861. This index was undertaken in the 1920s and 1930s and the library has no idea what the criteria were for inclusion. It is not just births, marriages and deaths, but what else? However this is a good starting point. A typical entry would be as below:-

> "MEIKLEHAM Professor D.S., MD, died 20 November 1849. (2nd December 1849 - 4/5)" - (i.e. the death notice appears in the 2nd December edition page 4 column 5.)

The Department holds a complete run of *Aberdeen Journal/Press & Journal,* 1747-1922, 1976 - on microfilm, the remainder in its original form. It also has runs of several other Aberdeen and north east newspapers. There is a self-service microfilm reader/printer.

Among the collections that the Library looks after is the MacBean collection of Jacobite material which is probably one of the best in the world for primary and secondary source material on this period.

The O'Dell collection includes train timetables, books on railways and trains as well as some wages books for this area in the nineteenth century. Further information on railway records as a source can be found in the Federation of Family History Society's publication *Was your Grandfather a Railwayman?*

There is also an extensive collection of pamphlets relating to many topics that can be found in the Thomson, Herald, King Collection. A card index by subject is available as a guide to these.

The Department houses the best collection of Estate Papers in the north east; these include the estate papers of the Ogilvie-Forbes family at Boyndlie, Gordon of Cairness and Buthlaw, Duff House/Montcoffer Lodge (Earls of Fife). There is more information in the "Reports and surveys of archives" series in the journal *Northern Scotland,* published by the Centre for Scottish Studies, University of Aberdeen. One of the manuscripts in the Archives is the original "List of pollable persons in the shire of Aberdeen, 1696", with a separate index compiled later, as well as the 1844 printed transcription.

Before going to any archive it is necessary to have a good idea of what you want and then it's as well to spend some time checking the library catalogue online to see if the archive can be of use. Perhaps the starting point for the family historian would be to search for a name or a place that you are interested in e.g.

LEITH - MS 2089 - Family of Leith, Account of the family of LEITH in Aberdeenshire - Alex W S Johnson.

LEITH - MS 2849 - Letters and papers of the LEITH families of Glenkindy and Freefield 17th-19th centuries.

Then you would wish to check the Manuscript (ms) Catalogue which gives greater detail of what is held. These 'ms' numbers can cover anything from a book, to a few papers, to 30-40 boxes of information. Once you check this and decide that there might be something there for you - fill out a request slip, hand it in, and wait. Sometimes a manuscript will not be available as it is in too poor a condition to be of use for research. Each time I visit the archives I am amazed by the amount of information that is held. Of course the main problem here, as with most archives, is there is no large index to the people contained in the manuscripts. However, half the fun of family history is in the "chase" and search through old documents.

In the Reading Room there are PCs with access to the main University Library catalogue, which includes their 3500 manuscript collections. If you do not find what you are looking for, you then use the old name sheaf catalogue (paper slips in small brown binders), then ask the staff about other printed catalogues and assistance. There are more detailed summary and descriptive lists for many of the manuscript collection, indicated by the note "List" in the catalogue entry. Unfortunately, as with most archives, there is no comprehensive index to the people referred to in the manuscripts. They also have survey lists of the National Register of Archives (Scotland)/NRA(S) relating to the north east and guides to various other local and national repositories, including the National Archives of Scotland, the India Office Library.

You can browse freely in the Local and O'Dell Collections and some of this material may be borrowed by registered readers. For other material that you want to consult, fill out a request card and hand it in to the Office. Most archival and some printed material will be fetched immediately. Other printed material is fetched at 9.15am, 10.15am and 2.00pm.

LIST OF POLLABLE PERSONS 1696 – LONMAY

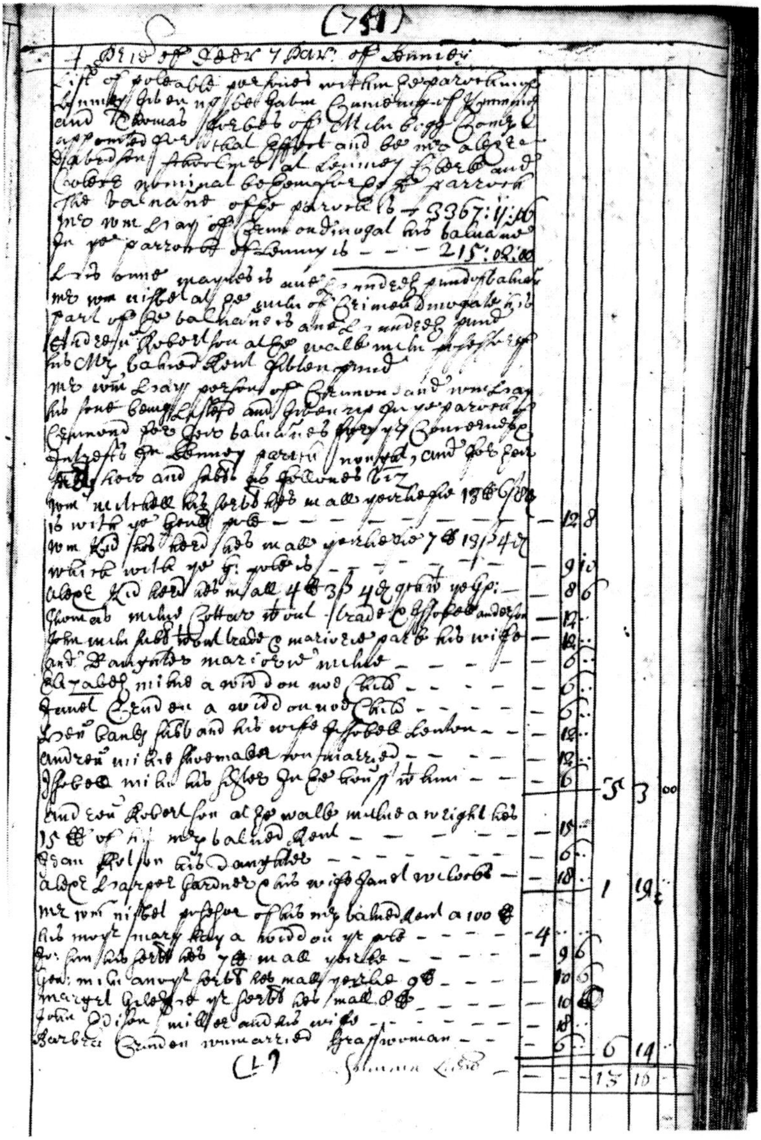

ABERDEEN & N.E. SCOTLAND FAMILY HISTORY SOCIETY

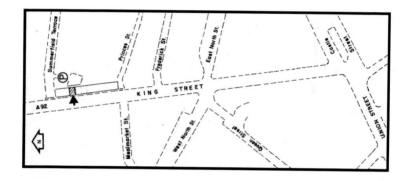

FAMILY HISTORY SHOP
158-164 KING STREET
ABERDEEN
AB24 5BD
Tel: (01224) 646323
Fax: (01224) 639096
Email: enquiries@anesfhs.org.uk
Website: http://www.anesfhs.org.uk

OPENING TIMES
MONDAY-FRIDAY   10.00am- 4.00pm
SATURDAY   9.00am- 1.00pm
TUESDAY&FRIDAY   7.00am-10.00pm
Closed on local and public holidays
No charge for members. £3.00 per hour charge non
members. No charge for advice and browsing.
Manned by volunteer staff.
Microfiche and Microfilm Printout facilities - 35p per page
Photocopies - 10p per A4 page
             - 20p per A3 page

PENCIL ONLY TO BE USED

SOME FACILITIES AT GROUND LEVEL

MEMBERSHIP RATES from 2008 are:

      One Person   £15.00
      Family   £20.00
(i.e. 2 named persons at 1 address)
Written enquiries dealt with, please send an SAE.

THE FAMILY HISTORY SHOP/RESEARCH CENTRE

This shop and research centre was opened in January 1987 by the Aberdeen and North East of Scotland Family History Society. It is funded by the members of the society, but is open to everyone. It was the first of its kind in Britain, if not the world.

The centre has microfiche readers and the following microfiche indexes - a complete set of the OPR index as published for Scotland, 1981 IGI for the whole of Scotland, 1988 IGI for the whole world, 1992 IGI for the UK and Commonwealth countries and the 1881 Census Index. As finance and availability allow, the Society is building up its stock, not all of them Scottish either, some come from England and all other parts of the world to where Scots emigrated.

As well as the indexes the Society has microfilm readers and microfilm of the OPRs and Census (1841-1891) for Scotland. As finance allows they will purchase more and more microfilms of original sources. There are also several networked computers with the IGI and all LDS disks (installed on hard drive), the pre-1855 burials index from OPRs for the North East, broadband Internet access, the full set of records at "Ancestry.com", access to ScotlandsPeople website (using vouchers available for purchase in the Centre) - and much else. CDs of many English census are also available.

Due to the tremendous success of the shop in the first few years of it opening the Society has had to move along the road to larger premises. Here there are better facilities not just for the staff but for the members. Although conditions for research can at times still be a little cramped the bookshop section of the centre is bright and airy with space to browse. Their bookshop is to be highly recommended and even if you cannot make it to the centre they will post any of their stock out to you. They have one of the best postal sales catalogues for family historians. It is updated in the middle of every year. If you wish to receive a copy please send an A5 SAE or 2 IRCs to them.

Reception, book shop and research centre of the Family History Shop.

One of the other great strengths of this centre is the Library which is continuously being extended. There are well over 3000 books of genealogical interest covering mostly Scotland but all parts of the world. These range from substantial textbooks to small localised pamphlets. The Society maintains an extensive exchange programme with other Societies worldwide and these Journals etc are worthy of a look on any visit. The library has been organised to make it as easy as possible for the amateur researcher to find material and can now be searched on-line in the Centre by author, title and keyword of interest.

- Reference - dictionaries, encyclopedias etc.
- Heraldry - Clans and Tartans - this also includes surnames
- Area research - split by county for the U.K.
- Genealogical Directories - members interests, worldwide
- Geography - atlases, maps, gazetteers
- Air/Military/Naval ancestors - also includes all seafarers
- Scotland - cultural and historical works of a general nature
- Scottish Counties - historical and descriptive works
- Scottish Families - individual family histories
- Biography - dictionaries, academic lists etc
- Overseas - emigration and other records from abroad
- Censuses - printed censuses and other lists
- Deaths, Monumental Inscriptions etc - also includes burial registers and wills
- Parish/Church registers - printed registers and also location lists
- Church History - includes individual churches as well as guides

The list above can only give the smallest flavour of all the sources that you can find in the centre. It is not only a must for anyone tracing north east ancestors but for anyone in the north-east tracing ancestors anywhere. There is something for everyone here whether your roots lie in Aberdeen or Zimbabwe, Caithness or Coventry, Wales or New South Wales.

Under this one roof there is the best genealogical research centre in the area, the best genealogical bookshop in Scotland (and perhaps even Britain) and one of the best genealogical reference libraries in Scotland. And if this is not enough, a visit to the centre will get you some of the best free advice around, let you meet other family historians and let you research in comfort. What more could a researcher want!

Outside the Family History Centre on King Street

ABERDEENSHIRE LIBRARY AND INFORMATION SERVICE
(A.L.I.S.)

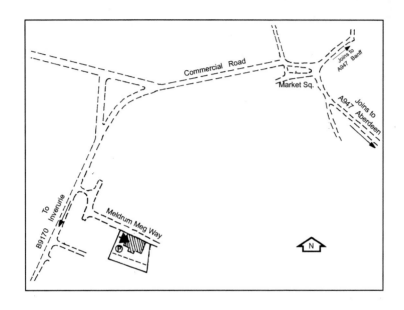

A.L.I.S.
MELDRUM MEG WAY
THE MEADOWS INDUSTRIAL ESTATE
OLDMELDRUM
ABERDEENSHIRE
AB51 0GN

Tel: 01651 871219/871220
Fax: 01651 872142
Email: local.studies@aberdeenshire.gov.uk
Websites: www.aberdeenshire.gov.uk/libraries
www.aberdeenshire.gov.uk/libraries/information/local studies.asp
Contact: Local Studies Librarian

OPENING TIMES
MONDAY - FRIDAY   9.00am-5.00pm
SATURDAY   9.00am-4.30pm

PLEASE MAKE AN APPOINTMENT

Photocopying facilities - 10p per page (A4/A3)
Fiche/Film printouts   - 10p per page

A.L.I.S.

The Aberdeenshire Library and Information Service is the 1996 descendant of The North East of Scotland Library Service which was set up at the time of local government reorganisation in the mid 1970s as the successor of the old local County Libraries Service. It runs the library services of Kincardine & Deeside, Gordon, and Banff and Buchan Districts leaving just Moray and Aberdeen City to run their own in the old Grampian Region. It has control of local branches to the extent of exchanging and buying stock, etc. The Local History Section has a wide collection of books and newspapers relating to the three districts that it covers. Each branch library holds material relating to its local area but the main reference collection is housed at the Administrative HQ at Oldmeldrum.

OPRs are held on microfilm for all parishes now within the boundaries of the three Districts and the microfiche index to the OPRs is held for the old counties of Aberdeen City, Aberdeenshire, Banffshire and Kincardineshire.

Fraserburgh branch library also holds microfilm copies of all the Old Parish Records for Banff and Buchan District and also the OPR Index for Aberdeenshire and Banffshire. Inverbervie, Inverurie, Kemnay, Peterhead, Stonehaven and Ellon all hold microfilm copies for the parishes in their immediate vicinity.

The International Genealogical Index (I.G.I.) latest edition, covering baptisms and marriages for the whole of Scotland, sorted by old county, from approximately the early 1500s to c.1875 is also held.

A.L.I.S. holds Census Records (microfilm of enumeration books) 1841, 1851, 1861, 1871, 1881 and 1891. The area covered is the same as the OPRs above, with some parishes just over the border in Moray District also being held (Botriphnie, Cabrach, Grange, Keith, Mortlach and Rothiemay).

Newspapers: All local newspapers have been kept by A.L.I.S.. since 1975. Before that, only certain newspapers are held, e.g. Huntly Express. Newspaper announcements of deaths and obituaries can be useful in family research.

They have just produced a very good guide to what sources they have for The Family Historian and this can be sent to you in return for the postage. The Staff at A.L.I.S. are very helpful and are very "tuned in" to family history.

All libraries and the local studies department have free internet access through the People's Network.

In the list on the next page of the A.L.I.S. branches, *denotes libraries with microfilm and microfiche resources. Please check with each library for opening hours and half days etc as each library has dramatically different opening days and hours.

A.L.I.S. BRANCHES

Aberchirder Library, 111 Main Street, Aberchirder, AB54 7TB	(01466) 780607
Aboyne Library, Community Centre, Bridgeview Road, Aboyne, AB34 5JN	(013398) 86004
Alford Library, Alford Academy, Murray Terrace, Alford, AB33 8PY	(019755) 63333
Ballater Library, Station Square, Ballater, AB35 5QB	(013397) 55628
Balmedie Library, Eigie Road, Balmedie, AB23 8YF	(01358) 742045
Banchory Library, Bridge Street, Banchory, AB31 5SU	(01330) 823784
Banff Library, High Street, Banff, AB45 1AE	(01261) 815052
Boddam Library, 26 Queens Road, Boddam, AB42 3AX	(01779) 473479
Bracoden Library, Bracoden School, Gamrie, AB45 3HA	(01261) 851539
Cairnbulg Library, Station Road, Cairnbulg, AB43 8WQ	(01346) 583121
Cruden Bay Library, Station Road, Cruden Bay, AB42 0NL	(01779) 812815
*Ellon Library, Station Road, Ellon, AB41 9AE	(01358) 720865
Fettercairn Library, Fettercairn School, Distillery Road, Fettercairn, AB30 1TH	(01561) 340442
*Fraserburgh Library, King Edward Street, Fraserburgh, AB43 9PN	(01346) 518197
*Huntly Library, Brander Library, The Square, Huntly, AB54 8BR	(01466) 792179
Insch Library, Insch Institute, Rannes Street, Insch, AB52 6JJ	(01464) 820841
*Inverbervie Library, Church Street, Inverbervie, DD10 0RU	(01561) 361690
*Inverurie Library, Town Hall, Market Place, Inverurie, AB51 3SN	(01467) 621619
*Kemnay Library, Kendal Road, Kemnay, AB51 5RN	(01467) 643906
Kintore Library, Kintore School, Castle Walk, Kintore, AB51 0RU	(01467) 634393
Laurencekirk Library, The Burgh Buildings, Johnston Street, Laurencekirk, AB30 1AN	(01561) 377298
*Macduff Library, 17 High Street, Macduff, AB44 1LR	(01261) 833289
Meldrum Library, Meldrum Academy, Colpy Road, Oldmeldrum, AB51 0NT	(01651) 871307
Mintlaw Library, Newlands Road, Mintlaw, AB42 5GP	(01771) 623366
New Pitsligo Library, 79 High Street, New Pitsligo, AB43 6NH	(01771) 653713
Newmachar Library, School Road, Newmachar, AB21 0WB	(01651) 862085
Newtonhill Library, Coastal Car Park, Newtonhill, AB39 3UL	(01569) 731825
*Peterhead Library, St Peter Street, Peterhead, AB42 1QD	(01779) 872554
Portlethen Library, Portlethen Academy, Bruntland Road, Portlethen, AB12 4QL	(01224) 786190
Portsoy Library, Aird Green, Portsoy, AB45 2RH	(01261) 843891
Rosehearty Library, Rosehearty School, Pitsligo Street, Rosehearty, AB43 7JL	(01346) 572001
*Stonehaven Library, Evan Street, Stonehaven, AB39 2ET	(01569) 762136
*Strichen Library, 59a Water Street, Strichen, AB43 6ST	(01771) 637347
Turriff Library, Grange Villa, The Square, Turriff, AB53 4AE	(01888) 562539
Westhill Library, Hay's Way, Westhill, AB32 6XZ	(01224) 741312
Whitehills Library, Loch Street, Whitehills, AB45 2LT	(01261) 861240

GRAMPIAN MAP

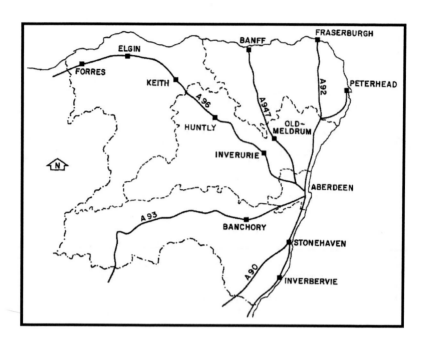

(This is a map of the previous local government administrative region known as Grampian).

_._._._._._.   Shows boundary of Region

------------   Shows district area boundaries within the Region

_ _ _   Main road links

ELGIN - Town Names

MORAY LOCAL HERITAGE CENTRE

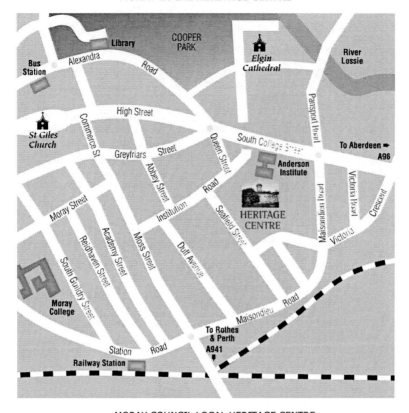

MORAY COUNCIL LOCAL HERITAGE CENTRE
OLD EAST END SCHOOL
INDUSTRIAL ROAD
ELGIN   IV30 1RP

Tel: (01343) 569011
Contact: Graeme Wilson
Email: heritage@moray.gov.uk
Website: www.moray.gov.uk

OPENING TIMES

MONDAY, WEDNESDAY, THURSDAY & FRIDAY: 10.00am- 5.00pm
TUESDAY : 10.00am- 8.00pm
SATURDAY: 10.00am-12.00pm

Closed Wednesdays from October to April.
Photocopying - 10p per A4 page, 20p per A3 page and 75p for microfilm printout.
Written Enquiries dealt with - please send an SAE or 2 x IRCs. The first half hour
of research is free but after that it is £12.50 per hour.

This historic school built in the 1830s and designed by Aberdeen architect Archibald Simpson is now the temporary home of local heritage centre for Moray. It specialises in its own particular area but also has general works of reference, family histories, etc. All the books are housed in the Reference Section. All the local history books are listed in the catalogue available at all the libraries and on the Moray Council's website. They have over 14,000 books and pamphlets one of the most extensive collections of books on Moray in the world.

They have the census records from 1841-1901 for their area and the OPRs as well, all available to be seen on microfilm. There is a collection of local newspapers from 1827 to date, over 20,000 local photos and 16,000 plus maps of the area.

Making use of Manpower Services Commission labour in the 1970s and 1980s they have compiled an index to the local newspapers (a mammoth job but well worth it for family historians). They index not just hatches, matches and dispatches but business, house sales, accidents, etc.

During 1978 and 1979 Elgin used another government backed scheme YOP (Youth Opportunity Programme) - school-leavers to survey and record the inscriptions in 52 local burial grounds. Each name that appears in an inscription has an index card showing brief details as below.

> "Erected by James Pirie in memory of his father JOHN PIRIE who died at Greenbog, 3.1.1863 aged 90. His wife MARGARET PETRIE died 23.5.1872 aged 97. The said JAMES PIRIE died 1.3.1888 aged 85. CHARLES PIRIE died 24.4.1915 aged 84. His wife MATHIESON died Greenbog 2.11.1905 aged 73"
> *(An inscription from Grange Churchyard in Banffshire)*

These have now all been transferred on to a computer index system, LIBINDX and there is public access via terminals in the library. As part of the LIBINDX system they have indexed all the deaths in the local OPRs as well. The work of the Moray Burial Ground Research Group (www.mbgrg.org) is also included in monumental inscriptions collection.

Over the years acquisitions to their microfilm stock have been such things as OPRs for Nairn county and the Valuation Rolls for Moray County from 1855-1900. As money allows, they will purchase the Valuation Rolls for Banffshire for the same time period. They have a lot of the post 1900 Valuation Rolls in stock already. They have also microfilmed the Poor Relief registers and School admission registers for their area. The originals are held in Aberdeen.

With the demise of Moray District Archives in the financial stringencies of the late 1990s all the research functions of these archives is now administered through the local heritage centre. Should you wish to access any of the archival material, first consult the catalogues to the archives which are held here, place your order and the material will be ready for you in 48 hours. This is not an ideal solution but space and staffing shortages mean this is the best service that can be provided at present. There is information from the 13th century to today. There are letter books, court records, town records, Kirk session records and so on. There is a wealth of material of use. There are also some 15,000 architect plans in the Wittet collection which dates from the mid 19th century to the 1960s. If your ancestors come from Moray this is the place for you!

MORAY DISTRICT LIBRARIES

Below is a list of the Libraries and Museums in this area

ABERLOUR LIBRARY, 94 High St	01340	871693
BUCKIE LIBRARY /MUSEUM, Cluny Place	01542	832121
BURGHEAD LIBRARY, Grant St.	01343	830186
CULLEN LIBRARY, Seafield Rd.	01542	841140
DUFFTOWN LIBRARY, Balvenie Street	01340	820272
DUFFTOWN MUSEUM, The Square	01340	820501
FINDOCHTY LIBRARY, Commercial St.	01542	832184
FOCHABERS LIBRARY, High St.	01343	821434
FORRES LIBRARY, Forres House, High Street	01309	672834
FORRES MUSEUM, Tolbooth	01309	673701
HOPEMAN LIBRARY, Forsyth St.	01343	830188
KEITH LIBRARY, Union Street	01542	882223
LOSSIEMOUTH LIBRARY, Town Hall Lane	01343	813334
PORTGORDON LIBRARY, Gordon St.	01542	835478
PORTKNOCKIE LIBRARY, Park St.	01542	841149
ROTHES LIBRARY, Seafield St.	01340	831281
TOMINTOUL LIBRARY,	01307	580271
TOMINTOUL MUSEUM, The Square	01307	580285

You can find sources for your family history anywhere – this memorial can be found on a wall of a ruined house at Aberdour beach in Aberdeenshire. Jane Thain is my husband's great grandmother.

Counties and Parishes of N.E. Scotland 1890-1975

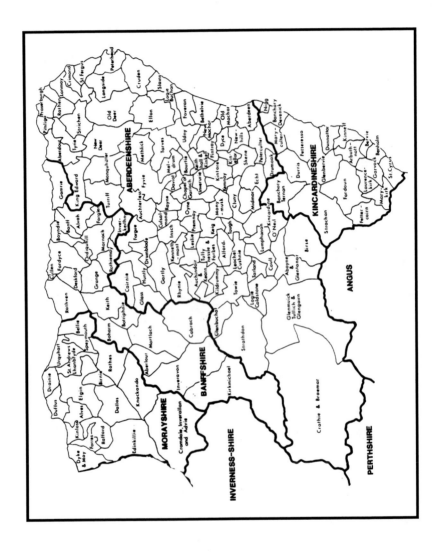

ABERDEEN CITY ARCHIVES - TOWN HOUSE

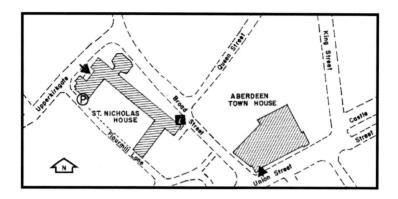

ABERDEEN CITY ARCHIVES
TOWN HOUSE
BROAD STREET
ABERDEEN   AB10 1AQ

TEL: (01224) 522513
FAX: (01224) 638556
Email: archives@aberdeencity.gov.uk
Website:
www.aberdeencity.gov.uk/acci/web/site/LocalHistory/RM/loc_Archiv
esHomePage.asp

CITY ARCHIVIST: Phil Astley

OPENING TIMES
WEDNESDAY - FRIDAY   9.30am - 4.30pm
(closed for lunch 12.30pm-1.30pm on occasions)

BY APPOINTMENT ONLY

Photocopying may be allowed at discretion of Archivist - 40p per page
Microfilm copies available at a small charge.
PENCIL ONLY TO BE USED
LIFT AVAILABLE
Enter by Union Street Entrance to Town House.
Written Enquiries dealt with - please send an SAE/ Limited research service
available at a cost of £7.50 per fifteen minutes.

The remit of this archive is to house the records relating exclusively to the present day Aberdeen City; this of course includes the Royal Burgh of Aberdeen, the Burgh of Old Aberdeen, and the Burgh of Woodside as well as a small number of private deposits. This might not sound much but in fact there is a vast amount of untapped genealogical information here. But as with most archives the information is mainly unindexed, often difficult to read and at times very fragile. Since 1995 there has been a project within the archives to index material (much of it eighteenth century) and put it on a computer system - CLIO. There is a search room which houses works of reference.

One of the first sources used by genealogists here is the registers of some of the burial grounds maintained by the District Council including St Peter's Cemetery 1769-1951, St Nicholas Kirkyard 1855-1925, (there are some early 19th century duplicate volumes) St Clements Kirkyard 1855-1927, John Knox Kirkyard 1837-1894 and Old Machar Kirkyard 1863-1906. A typical entry from St Peter's is below.

> "HENRY CHESER son of PETER CHESER, brushmaker - Aberdeen
> Age 1 buried at a depth of 5 feet on Dec 13th 1851. Charge 2/1d."

The more modern graveyard information for the Aberdeen area is held in St Nicholas House by the Department of Leisure and Recreation on the First Floor. They have the same phone number as the Archives and the Registrar. To visit them you enter by the Broad Street entrance to St Nicholas House (see page 3).

This is only the tip of the iceberg for information of use to family historians. There are Stent (tax rolls in existence from the 15th century), there are the Police rate assessment rolls for Aberdeen for 1795-1860 (not every year), for Old Aberdeen for 1832-1850 and 1881-1891 and for Woodside for 1882-1886.

There are registers of admissions as burgesses of guild and of trade from the 17th century to the 20th century. There are also Registers of Indentures of Apprentices from 1632-1878 which is incomplete but could contain such information as name of apprentice, place of origin, father's name, master's name, date of indenture and the premium. (Some of these have been published).

Earlier records include such material as Council Registers from 1398, Baillie Court Books 1572-1780, Burgh Register of Sasines 1484-1809 etc.

Aberdeen St Nicholas and St Clement (Church of Scotland) Kirk Session records, as well as Aberdeen Presbytery records from 1925-1975 are held under charge and superintendence from the Keeper of the Records of Scotland. Also surviving historical records of Aberdeen Congregational Churches (1798-1980) are housed here.

A much fuller but out-of-date list of records is contained in Part IV of *Charters Relating to the Burgh of Aberdeen* by P J Anderson (Aberdeen 1890). In the footnotes to this book mention is made of material published e.g. Entries of Admission of Burgesses are in *New Spalding Club Miscellany Vol.1*.

ABERDEEN CITY ARCHIVES – OLD ABERDEEN

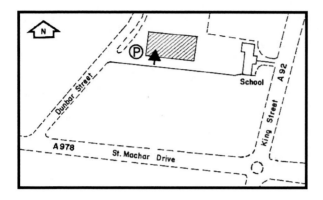

ABERDEEN CITY ARCHIVES
OLD ABERDEEN HOUSE
DUNBAR STREET
ABERDEEN   AB24 3UJ

TEL: (01224) 481775
FAX: (01224) 495830
Email: archives@aberdeencity.gov.uk
www.aberdeencity.gov.uk/acci/web/site/LocalHistory/RM/loc_ArchivesHomePage.
asp

OPENING TIMES
MONDAY - WEDNESDAY: 9.30am-1.00pm, 2.00pm-4.30pm
(Closed Lunchtime 1 - 2)

BY APPOINTMENT ONLY
PENCIL ONLY TO BE USED
Photocopying can be provided at discretion of the staff - 40p per page

ALL FACILITIES ON GROUND LEVEL
Postal enquiries can be dealt with - please include an SAE/ Limited research
service available at a cost of £7.50 per fifteen minutes.

Opened in 1986 in part of the ground floor of what was Old Aberdeen School, this is the best archive for facilities in the area because it has been designed for the purpose. The search room and the store are side by side and the archivist is able to access material quickly for the researcher.

The search room is large and can hold more researchers than the staff could cope with. Within this area are held the catalogues of material in the custody of the archivist as well as several indexes that have been done by volunteers, e.g. Worral's Directory for Banffshire, Kincardineshire and Aberdeenshire 1877, and the Valuation Roll for Banffshire and Kincardineshire 1878/1879.

There is information here from the early 17th century to the present covering the geographical area of Aberdeenshire as well as some concerning Aberdeen City.

SOME OF THE SOURCES FOR FAMILY HISTORY

1.   THE POOR AND THEIR RELATIVES

- Minutes and Registers of Parochial Boards 1845-1894 and Parish Councils 1894-1930 (ms. index of Registers).

2.   TEACHERS AND PUPILS

- Admission Registers of Pupils and School Log Books 1864-1975 (ms. some volumes indexed but no general index).
- Minutes 1873-1919 of Parish and Burgh School Boards (ms. not indexed).
- Minutes 1919-1975 of City and County Education Authorities (printed with volume indexes but no general index).

3.   PROPERTY OWNERS, TENANTS AND OCCUPIERS

- Valuation Rolls - printed volumes arranged by county and parish, but not indexed; issued every year from 1855 but copies of some early volumes survive only in the Scottish Record Office, Edinburgh which holds a complete set for Scotland.
- Aberdeen City 1855/56 - 1974/75.
- Aberdeen County (excluding city) 1859/60, 1864/65, 1869/70, 1874/75, 1879/80-1974/75.
- Banff County 1877/78, 1891/92-1974/75.
- Kincardine County 1862/63, 1869/70, 1873/74, 1878/79, 1881/82-1974/75

4.   ELECTORS

REGISTERS, arranged by polling districts, printed, not indexed - complete series held by Scottish Record Office, Edinburgh. Aberdeen City 1946;1950-1974, Aberdeen County 1918-1974; Banff County 1939, 1950-1974;   Kincardine County 1918-1974

5.   COUNCILLORS AND LOCAL GOVERNMENT OFFICIALS

County Council Minutes etc

Aberdeenshire 1713-1975, printed indexed from 1890, but index only by volume. No general index.
Banffshire 1772-1975 printed from 1890, not indexed.

<u>Town Council Minutes etc</u> on loan from Banff and Buchan and Gordon District Councils, ms not indexed.

Aberchirder	1890-1964	Inverurie	1797-1975	Portsoy	1889-1964
Banff	1694-1965	Kintore	1747-1975	Rosehearty	1811-1964
Ellon	1893-1975	Macduff	1783-1960	Turriff	1858-1968
Fraserburgh	1840-1966	Oldmeldrum	1893-1975		
Huntly	1834-1975	Peterhead	1820-1965		

For Family historians the two sources most used in the archive would be the Poor relief information and School records both of which give a picture of life in the north east in the 19th century . An example of the type of information that can be accessed is:

PETERHEAD POOR'S ROLL 1848

MARGARET CORDINER living the Ronheads, aged 64, widow of Charles Alexander. Born in Cruden - only source of income curing and selling fish. Her family assists partly - Margaret (45), Ann (39), Robert (35), Janet (33), Catherine(28).
Given 16/- yearly.

MARY SOUTTAR in the Ronheads, aged 73, widow of William BUCHAN born in Peterhead. Only source of income curing and selling fish when they can be got. Partially disabled by old age. Admitted to the Poor's Roll on 24/5/1835. Got 1/- weekly and house rent free.

Not only are there records of who got what, there are also at times the application books and these include those who did not get any aid. The applications, the registers and the children's list have all been indexed by members of the Family History Society and these are lodged in the Archives and in the Family History Shop.

CULSALMOND SCHOOL ADMISSION REGISTER 1874

NORTHERN HEALTH SERVICES ARCHIVES

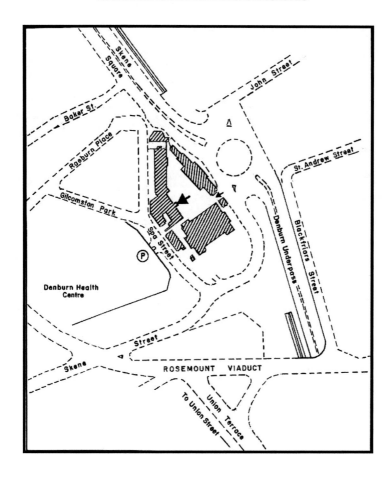

NORTHERN HEALTH SERVICES ARCHIVES
VICTORIA PAVILION
WOOLMANHILL HOSPITAL
ABERDEEN   AB25 1LD

TEL: 01224 555562 (There is an answering machine)
EMAIL: f.watson@nhs.net
ARCHIVIST: Miss Fiona Watson

OPENING HOURS
Office hours, by appointment. There is space for only 2 researchers at a time.

PLEASE PHONE IN ADVANCE if disabled access is required.
PENCIL ONLY TO BE USED.
Telephone, email and postal enquiries dealt with - please include a SAE.

Health Board records are a source not often used by family historians but there is a wealth of information to be found there (see page 36 for example) and often nowhere else. We are lucky in Aberdeen to have one of the four Health Board archivists in the country. (The others are in Dumfries, Edinburgh and Glasgow).Details of the archives' holding will be found in the Scottish Archive Network online catalogue www.scan.org.uk by searching under Northern Health Service Archive in the Repository field.

Types of hospital covered by the archives include:-

GENERAL HOSPITALS e.g. Aberdeen Royal Infirmary whose records date back to the 1740s.

PSYCHIATRIC HOSPITALS e.g. Royal Cornhill Hospital in Aberdeen which is the oldest of its kind in Grampian, opening on its present site in 1800.

SOME POORHOUSES: Records of those poorhouses originally set up following the 1845 Poor Law Amendment Act but which later became National Health Service hospitals are often to be found in Health Board archives. In Grampian these are the Buchan Combination Poorhouse (Maud Hospital), Kincardineshire Combination Poorhouse (Woodcot Hospital, Stonehaven) and Aberdeen's Oldmill Poorhouse (Woodend Hospital).

INFECTIOUS DISEASE HOSPITALS: These started mainly in the late 19th century. The City Hospital in Aberdeen opened in 1877, and others include Ellon (1888), Inverurie (1897), Stonehaven (1903) and Dufftown (1905).

The main sources of information about patients are admission registers and case notes. Due to the confidential nature of such records they are closed for either 75 or 100 years. Admission registers can include such information as patient's name and parish, his disease, dates of stay in hospital and, by the mid 19th century, also his age, occupation and native place. The amount of detail does vary from hospital to hospital. Where case notes have survived there will sometimes be additional information about the patient's background e.g. the cause or duration of his current illness.

Psychiatric patient records have even more detail as after 1857 they include lunacy forms i.e. petitions to the Sheriff seeking to have the patient admitted to hospital. These forms give many personal details including the next of kin and the names of any relatives known to have had mental illness.

Staff information is also held. Appointments and resignations of senior staff are usually noted in minute books and from the late 19th century there are often nursing and other staff registers. In addition to the basic employment details these can sometimes contain training details, previous experience and posts held after qualifying. For doctors there are the published Medical Register and Medical Directory to check first.

Useful published sources that can help plan any trip to the Archives are detailed below:

Fiona Watson, *In Sickness and in Health: Health Care in Grampian* (Aberdeen 1987)

S. Smith & M. Wilson, *Aberdeen Royal Infirmary Deaths Recorded 1743-1897* (4 vols)

KINCARDINESHIRE POOR'S HOUSE REGISTER OF ADMISSIONS - 1867

KINCARDINESHIRE POOR'S HOUSE REGISTER OF ADMISSIONS - 1867

DATE ADMITTED	NAME	AGE	OCCUPATION	CAUSE FOR ADMISSION	PARISH TO WHICH CHARGEABLE	DATE OF LEAVING	REMARKS
Aug 28	William Gregory	61	Weaver	Want of Arm	Fetteresso	6 Sep 1874	Died of Paralysis
	George Marshall	68	Farm Servant	Gen' Debility	Maryculter	22 Nov 1869	Died of Disease of Heart and Dropsy
Aug 29	James Main	67	Shoemaker	Old Age etc	Fetteresso	22 Nov 1870	Died of Heart Disease and Asthma
Aug 29	David Cowie	71	Labourer	Paralytic	Fetteresso	22 Mar 1871	Died of Bronchial Affection
Aug 30	Janet McGregor	42	Domestic Servant	Lame Arm	Dunnottar	29 Nov 1878	Died of Psthisis
	John Boyd	8	None	Destitution	Dunnottar	31 May 1871	Sent to Service
Aug 31	Jane Durno	17	Millworker	Pregancy	Banchory Devenick	10 Mar 1868	Voluntary
Sep 2	Isabella Paul	37	Weaving	Blindness	Fetteresso	5 Jun 1868	Voluntary
	George Paul	6	None	Dependant	Fetteresso	5 June 1868	Dependant
Sep 13	Widow Stephen or Hunter	63	None	Bedridden	Dunnottar	3 Dec 1869	Taken charge of by daughter
Sep 14	David Ross	78	Wright	Frailty	Strachan	8 Jun 1868	Died of General Debility
Sep 16	James Burnett	45	Shepherd	Ill Health	Fetteresso	18 Jul 1868	Gone to Service
Sep 23	Christina McIntyre	24	Millworker	Child	Dunnottar	25 Sep 1867	Could not stop in house without tobacco
	Isabella McIntyre	2mths		Dependant	Dunnottar	25 Sep 1867	Taken away by mother

Reproduced by kind permission of Northern Health Services Archive

Produced by kind permission of Northern Health Services Archives